"Jewish Women Are Vessels of Love, Light, and Life."
Eve Paikoff

SHABBAT BLESSING

A Silent Blessing for Centuries
Is Blessed with Two New Melodies

Traditional Melody & Hassidic Melody for Voice & Piano

YEHE RATZON L'FANECHA

World Renowned Israeli Composer Ronn Yedidia
Vocals By Mezzo-Soprano Sharon Esther Lampert

Yehe Ratzon L'fanecha: May It Be Your Will To Show Favor

Thinking Especially of You

Gift Card

Date:

To:

From:

Message:

Music, Cantorial Music, Religion, Judaism, Shabbat Blessings

SHABBAT BLESSING
A Silent Blessing for Centuries
Is Blessed with Two New Melodies
Traditional Melody & Hassidic Melody for Voice & Piano

©1995 ©2015 ©2025 by Sharon Esther Lampert. All Rights Reserved. No part of this book may be used or reproduced in any manner whatsoever without written permission except in the case of brief quotations embodied in critical articles and reviews.

KADIMAH PRESS
GIFTS OF GENIUS

KADIMAH PRESS books may be purchased for education, business, or sales promotional use.
Phone: 561-888-0313

3 EDITIONS:
Hardcover ISBN: 979-8-3483-1749-2
Paperback ISBN: 979-8-3483-1766-9
e-book ISBN: 979-8-3483-1767-6
2025 Library of Congress Catalog Card Number: 2025900209

1995-2015 Library of Congress Catalog Card Number: 2007902026
Copyright: July 6, 1998 #PAu2-373-742
Comissioned Music Composition Contract Agreement: 6/20/1995

Fan Mail:
sharon@sharonestherlampert.com

Websites:
www.SharonEstherLampert.com
www.WorldFamousPoems.com

Book Design and Interior and Editor: Sharon Esther Lampert

For Orders and Distribution:
Ingram, 1 Ingram Blvd. La Vergne, TN 37086-3629
Phone: 615-793-5000,
Fax orders: 615-287-6990

First Edition

Manufactured in the United States of America

SHABBAT BLESSING
A Silent Blessing for Centuries
Is Blessed with Two New Melodies
Traditional Melody & Hassidic Melody for Voice & Piano

KADIMAH PRESS
GIFTS OF GENIUS
Jerusalem, Israel

Biographical Note

My First Note to God

As is the tradition, I left my first handwritten note in the Wailing Wall on my first trip to Israel with my parents, on the occassion of my brother Benjamin's Bar Mitzvah in Jerusalem; and to visit my first cousins Bunya and Yankle Lampert and their sons and my second cousins Israel and Georah in Ramat Gan, Israel.

For Your Information

The Kotel or the Western Wall (Kotel ha'Maarav) is not an actual wall of the Second Temple, it is a retaining wall to the outer courtyard near the Temple built many years after the Temple.

1.
The construction of the Western Wall itself was started as part of King Herod's renovations of the Temple Mount that began in the 1st century BCE.

2.
After the destruction of the Second Temple in 70 CE, all four of the retaining walls survived.

3.
Both because of its proximity to the Holy of Holies and accessibility, the Western Wall became a place of yearning, mourning, and tears for the Jewish people.

4.
Jewish law dictates that Jews should pray facing the Kotel, no matter where they are in the world, and this is why Jews face east (Kitzur Shulchan Aruch 18:10).

Dedication

My First Note to God

"Dear God,
I am not asking for help.
I am offering to be of help.
I am at your service."

SHARON ESTHER LAMPERT
SEE THE WORLD THROUGH THE EYES OF A CREATIVE GENIUS

SCIENTIST, ARTIST, EDUCATOR, AND THEOLOGIAN
Prodigy, Prophet, Philosopher, Paladin of Education, Performer,
PHOTON SUPERHERO, Psychobiologist, Physicist, and PIN-UP

My Father Abraham Lampert's Nickname Was

BEZALEL
"In the Shadow of God"

The Chief Architect of the Covenant
I Inherited the Blessing.
Exodus: 31:3

By Abraham Lampert
Shabbat Candlesticks Made of Cyprus Stone
Made in the Cyprus Internment Camp, 1948
Highlight: **Golda Meir** visited the Cyprus Detention Camp
The ship **AF AL PI CHEN** is in the Haifa Museum
A Russian Holocaust survivor, my father lived in Israel for 10 years.
Exhibited at **The Museum of Jewish Heritage**:
A Living Memorial to the Holocaust
36 Battery Park, NYC

Yehe Ratzon L'fanecha: May It Be Your Will To Show Favor

Table of Contents

YEHE RATZON L'FANECHA
THE SILENT SHABBAT CANDLE LIGHTING BLESSING

Hebrew

English

Transliteration

Hebrew Liturgical

Traditional Shabbat Blessing Melody
(Voice & Piano)

Hassidic Melody for SHABBAT Chorus
(Voice & Piano)

Original Handwritten Manuscripts of Ronn Yedidia

About Us

WORLD RENOWNED ISRAELI COMPOSER AND PIANIST
RONN YEDIDIA

PRINCESS KADIMAH: VOCALIST AND 8TH PROPHETESS OF ISRAEL
SHARON ESTHER LAMPERT

Silent Shabbat Blessing For Centuries Is Blessed by Two New Melodies

YEHE RATZON L'FANECHA
THE SILENT SHABBAT CANDLE LIGHTING BLESSING

HEBREW

יְהִי רָצוֹן מִלְּפָנֶיךָ יהוה אֱלֹהַי וֵאלֹהֵי אֲבוֹתַי, שֶׁתְּחוֹנֵן אוֹתִי
(וְאֶת אִישִׁי ׀ וְאֶת בָּנַי ׀ וְאֶת בְּנוֹתַי ׀ וְאֶת אָבִי ׀ וְאֶת אִמִּי)
וְאֶת כָּל קְרוֹבַי, וְתִתֶּן לָנוּ וּלְכָל יִשְׂרָאֵל חַיִּים טוֹבִים וַאֲרוּכִים, וְתִזְכְּרֵנוּ בְּזִכְרוֹן טוֹבָה וּבְרָכָה, וְתִפְקְדֵנוּ בִּפְקֻדַּת יְשׁוּעָה וְרַחֲמִים, וּתְבָרְכֵנוּ בְּרָכוֹת גְּדוֹלוֹת, וְתַשְׁלִים בָּתֵּינוּ, וְתַשְׁכֵּן שְׁכִינָתְךָ בֵּינֵינוּ, וְזַכֵּנִי לְגַדֵּל בָּנִים וּבְנֵי בָנִים, חֲכָמִים וּנְבוֹנִים, אוֹהֲבֵי יהוה, יִרְאֵי אֱלֹהִים, אַנְשֵׁי אֱמֶת, זֶרַע קֹדֶשׁ, בַּיהוה דְּבֵקִים, וּמְאִירִים אֶת הָעוֹלָם בַּתּוֹרָה וּבְמַעֲשִׂים טוֹבִים, וּבְכָל מְלֶאכֶת עֲבוֹדַת הַבּוֹרֵא. אָנָּא שְׁמַע אֶת תְּחִנָּתִי בָּעֵת הַזֹּאת, בִּזְכוּת שָׂרָה וְרִבְקָה וְרָחֵל וְלֵאָה אִמּוֹ־תֵינוּ. וְהָאֵר נֵרֵנוּ שֶׁלֹּא יִכְבֶּה לְעוֹלָם וָעֶד, וְהָאֵר פָּנֶיךָ וְנִוָּשֵׁעָה, אָמֵן.

YEHE RATZON L'FANECHA
THE SILENT SHABBAT CANDLE LIGHTING BLESSING

ENGLISH

May it be Your will Lord, my G-d and G-d of my forefathers, that You show favour to me (my husband | my sons | my daughters | my father | my mother) and all of my relatives; and that You grant us and all Israel a good long life; that You remember us with beneficent memory and blessing;

that You consider us with a consideration of salvation and compassion; that You bless us with great blessings; that You make our households complete; that you cause your presence to dwell among us.

Privilege me to raise children and grandchildren who are wise and understanding, who will love Hashem and fear G-d, people of truth, holy offspring attached to G-d, who will illuminate the world with Torah and good deeds and with every labour in the service of the creator.

Please, hear my supplication at this time, in the merit of Sarah, Rebecca, Rachel and Leah, our Mothers, and cause our light to illuminate that it be not extinguished forever, and let Your countenance shine so that we are saved.

Amen.

Silent Shabbat Blessing For Centuries Is Blessed by Two New Melodies

YEHE RATZON L'FANECHA
THE SILENT SHABBAT CANDLE LIGHTING BLESSING

TRANSLITERATION

Y'he Ratzon Milfanechah, Adonai Elohai Vei-lohei Avotai,

Sheh-t'chonein Oti (V'et Ishi | V'et Banai | V'et B'notai | V'et Avi V'et Imi)

V'et Kol K'rovai, V'titein Lanu Ul'chol Yisrael Chayim Tovim V'aruchim; V'tizk'reinu B'zichron Tova Uvracha; V'tifk'deinu Bifkudat Y'shua V'rachamim; Ut'varecheinu B'rachot G'dolot; V'tashlim Bateinu; V'tashkein Sh'chinatcha Beineinu. V'zakeini L'gadel Banim Uvnei Vanim Chachamim Un'vonim, Ohavei Adonai, Yirei Elohim, Anshei Emet, Zerah Kodesh, BaDonai D'veikim, Um'irim Et Ha-olam BaTorah Uv'ma-asim Tovim, Uv'chol M'lechet Avodat Haborei. Anah Sh'ma Et T'chinati Ba-eit Hazot, Bizchut Sarah V'Rivka V'Rachel V'Leah Imoteinu, V'ha-er Neireinu Shelo Yichbeh L'olam Va-ed, V'ha-er Panechah V'nivashei-ah. Amen."

Yehe Ratzon L'fanecha: May It Be Your Will To Show Favor

YEHE RATZON L'FANECHA
THE SILENT SHABBAT CANDLE LIGHTING BLESSING

HEBREW LITURGICAL

יהִי רָצוֹן מִלְפָנֶיךָ ה' אֱלֹהַי וֵאלֹהֵי אֲבוֹתַי שֶׁתְּחוֹנֵן אוֹתִי וְאֶת כָּל קְרוֹבַי, וְתִתֶּן לָנוּ וּלְכָל יִשְׂרָאֵל חַיִּים טוֹבִים וַאֲרוּכִים, וְתִזְכְּרֵנוּ בְּזִכְרוֹן טוֹבָה וּבְרָכָה, וְתִפְקְדֵנוּ בִּפְקֻדַּת יְשׁוּעָה וְרַחֲמִים וּתְבָרְכֵנוּ בְּרָכוֹת גְּדוֹלוֹת, וְתַשְׁלִים בָּתֵּינוּ, וְתַשְׁכֵּן שְׁכִינָתְךָ בֵּינֵינוּ, וְזַכֵּנִי לְגַדֵּל בָּנִים וּבְנֵי בָנִים חֲכָמִים וּנְבוֹנִים אוֹהֲבֵי ה' יִרְאֵי אֱלֹהִים אַנְשֵׁי אֱמֶת, זֶרַע קֹדֶשׁ בַּה' דְּבֵקִים וּמְאִירִים אֶת הָעוֹלָם בַּתּוֹרָה וּבְמַעֲשִׂים טוֹבִים וּבְכָל מְלֶאכֶת עֲבוֹדַת הַבּוֹרֵא. אָנָּא שְׁמַע אֶת תְּחִנָּתִי בָּעֵת הַזֹּאת, בִּזְכוּת שָׂרָה וְרִבְקָה וְרָחֵל וְלֵאָה אִמּוֹתֵינוּ. וְהָאֵר נֵרֵנוּ עִלָּא יִכְבֶּה לְעוֹלָם וָעֶד וְהָאֵר פָּנֶיךָ וְנִוָּשֵׁעָה אָמֵן

Silent Shabbat Blessing For Centuries Is Blessed by Two New Melodies

YEHE RATZON L'FANECHA
Shabbat Candle Lighting Blessing
Traditional Melody for Voice & Piano

World Renowned Israeli Composer and Pianist
Ronn Yedidia

Yehe Ratzon L'fanecha: May It Be Your Will To Show Favor

Silent Shabbat Blessing For Centuries Is Blessed by Two New Melodies

Yehe Ratzon L'fanecha: May It Be Your Will To Show Favor

Silent Shabbat Blessing For Centuries Is Blessed by Two New Melodies

Original Handwritten Manuscripts of Ronn Yedidia

Yehe Ratzon L'fanecha: May It Be Your Will To Show Favor

Original Handwritten Manuscripts of Ronn Yedidia

Silent Shabbat Blessing For Centuries Is Blessed by Two New Melodies

YEHE RATZON L'FANECHA
Shabbat Candle Lighting Blessing
Hassidic Melody for Voice & Piano

World Renowned Israeli Composer and Pianist
Ronn Yedidia

Yehe Ratzon L'fanecha: May It Be Your Will To Show Favor

Silent Shabbat Blessing For Centuries Is Blessed by Two New Melodies

Yehe Ratzon L'fanecha: May It Be Your Will To Show Favor

© Sharon Esther Lampert, www.poetryjewels.com, 1996

Silent Shabbat Blessing For Centuries Is Blessed by Two New Melodies

Original Handwritten Manuscripts of Ronn Yedidia

Yehe Ratzon L'fanecha: May It Be Your Will To Show Favor

Original Handwritten Manuscripts of Ronn Yedidia

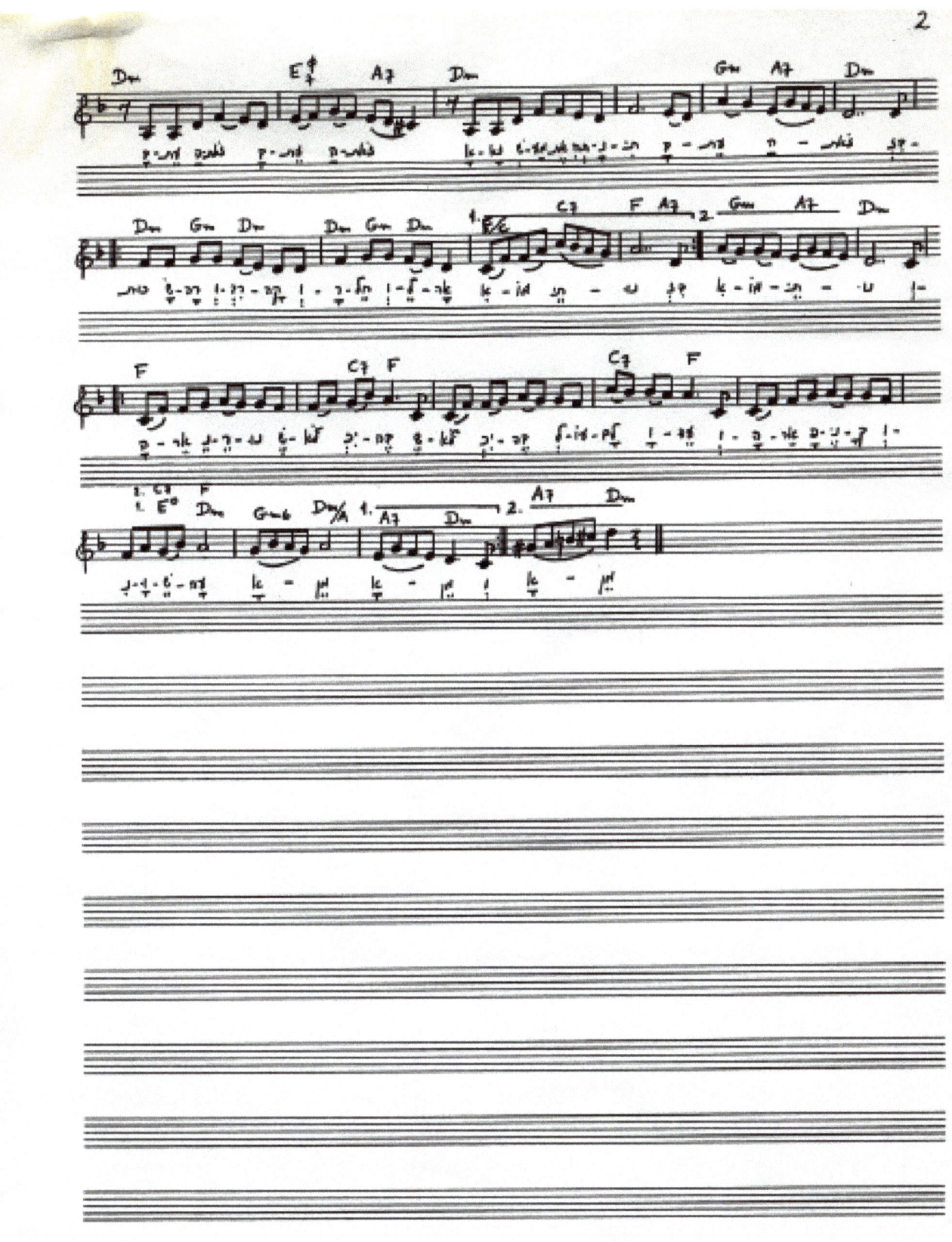

Silent Shabbat Blessing For Centuries Is Blessed by Two New Melodies

About the World Renowned Israeli Composer
Ronn Yedidia

Ronn Yedidia's compositions have galvanized the attention of performing artists worldwide during the last two decades. His works have been featured in major concert halls and documented on film, radio and television. He has won high critical acclaim from leading newspapers around the world, as both composer and pianist.

Born in 1960 in Tel Aviv, Israel, he began his musical career as a child prodigy pianist, winning 1st Prize at the Young Concert Artists' Competition of Israel at the age of eight. His main teacher and mentor was Israel's first lady of the piano, Pnina Salzman, who herself was a protege of Alfred Cortot. Active as a performer for many years, Ronn decided at the age of 15 to shift his attention towards composition. In 1984 he entered the Juilliard School from which he holds a Doctor of Musical Arts Degree in composition. During his studies there under David Diamond and Milton Babbitt he received all the major prizes in composition, including the **Lincoln Center Scholarship,** the **Irving Berlin Scholarship**, the **Henry Mancini Prize**, and the **Richard Rodgers Scholarship**. He also won the **Juilliard Composition Competition** twice – in 1987 & 1989 – and as a result had his works performed at the Juilliard Theater and at Alice Tully Hall.

Soon after Ronn Yedidia's arrival at Juilliard, he was discovered by Sony Classical's Executive Producer, Thomas Frost, who produced a recording of his Fusion-Jazz works. In 1985, his Second Piano Sonata was selected for radio exchange between Israel and numerous countries around the world. In 1987 he was presented on Israeli Television as **Discovery of the Year in Classical Music,** performing his Third Piano Sonata, "Outcries."

Yehe Ratzon L'fanecha: May It Be Your Will To Show Favor

Ronn Yedidia's awards include the 2006 San Antonio International Piano Competition Commission for which he composed his Rhapsody – which was performed by all finalists of the competition; 2002 commissions from the Zamir Chorale and from the Oklahoma City Community Fund; a 1998 America-Israel Cultural Foundation Commission; a 1997 BMI Grant; 1997 Honors at the John Lennon International Songwriting contest; a 1992 New York Foundation for the Arts Fellowship; First Prize at the 1992 Chicago Ensemble's First Discover America Competition; First Prize at the 1991 New Sounds Competition in Louisville, Kentucky; an ASCAP Grant in 1990 for his Piano Sonata No. 3, "Outcries"; the Milton Babbitt Prize in 1989 and the 1988 Brian Israel Award.

The Seattle Chamber Music Society selected Ronn Yedidia to be its first-ever commissioned composer – on the occasion of its 26th Summer Festival which was held in Seattle during July & August, 2007. He composed a Trio for clarinet, cello and piano which was premiered at the festival by clarinetist Alexander Fiterstein, cellist Amit Peled, and pianist Alon Goldstein, and the press cited him for his bravery of composing in the romantic vein of 19th and 20th-century masters, while keeping his authenticity and managing to avoid cliche or pastiche of old mannerisms.

In the fall of 2009, Ronn Yedidia was appointed Resident Composer of "The Concert Meister Series" held at the Baruch Performing Arts Center in Manhattan. The series presents solo & chamber appearances by concertmasters and principal instrumentalists of some of the world's leading orchestras, such as the Vienna Philharmonic, the Berlin Philharmonic and the Israel Philharmonic Orchestra, and Yedidia's compositions are featured amongst traditional works on each program.

Ronn Yedidia's compositions have been broadcast on NPR as well as New York radio stations WQXR, WNYC, WNCN & WFUV and he has been featured on NBC & WOR television networks in the U.S. and on both KBS-TV and MBC-TV in South Korea. His works have received critical acclaim throughout the world. The Los Angeles Times has cited "Yedidia's wealth of invention and compact construction" in the Concerto for Piano, Electronic Instruments, Choir & Orchestra, describing it as "...a recasting of the Lisztian virtuoso Piano Concerto in a contemporary medium," and concluding that "... the composer has his own voice."

In 1994, Ronn Yedidia was invited by Thomas Frost and Wanda Toscanini-Horowitz to edit and record the unpublished piano compositions of the legendary pianist Vladimir Horowitz. Ronn's friendship with the great Israeli composer, the late Alexander Argov gave rise to the project in which he has been the editor and transcriber of a collection of songs by Argov, which has been published by GIA Productions in Israel.

In 1993, Ronn founded the concert series 20th Century Music & On which presents a diverse cross-section of contemporary music in New York, and for which he has been composing his recent large-scale chamber works.

Between 1993 and 1998 he served as Composer in Residence and Chairman of the Piano Department at the Bloomingdale House of Music in Manhattan. A piano pedagogue of note, his students have been recognized in numerous competitions and festivals throughout the U.S. and Europe. Between 2001 and 2004, he served as Vice President and Program Director of the Piano Teachers Congress of New York. Between the summers of 2003 and 2006, he served as a Piano and Composition Professor at the Puigcerda Festival of Classical Music – situated in the Catalan region of Spain and France.

Silent Shabbat Blessing For Centuries Is Blessed by Two New Melodies

Ronn Yedidia is regarded by many also as an accordion virtuoso. He started playing the accordion at the age of 6 under the direction of his father, Moshe Yedidia – who was a well-known poet, actor, and accordionist in Israel. Since 2001, he has been involved in the creation of several klezmer ensembles in the New York area, both as an accordionist and as a musical arranger. In the fall of 2008, he formed the ensemble DanzaNova which arranges, composes & performs virtuoso ethnic music from all over the world with a special emphasis on dance. DanzaNova released its debut CD (entitled "Desert Winds") in the spring of 2015.

Another project in which Ronn has been involved as an accordionist as well as a composer & arranger is Polkastra, a virtuoso modern polka ensemble led by violinist Lara St. John and polka-composer Daniel Lapp. Polkastra's CD, "Apolkalypse Now," has hit the #1 spot on iTunes' World Music category during the month of June, 2009, and Ronn's "Celtic Kalkadunga Polka" featuring didgeridoo master William Barton – has been the most downloaded tune from the album on iTunes. Another track of Ronn's, the "Flying Gypsy Polka" has been distinguished by Allan Kozinn of the New York Times as "a vigorous accordion workout," and "the musicianship of the band – first rate !"

A more recent facet in Ronn's musical life has been popular-style singing. He has composed more than 150 songs and has had several writers adapt lyrics to them. Most of those lyrics are in Hebrew. On May 5, 2007, he appeared for the first time as a singer with a band – featuring 20 of his songs in a special concert held at Tel Aviv's famous pop music venue – Tzavta 1.

A more recent facet in Ronn's musical life has been popular-style singing. He has composed more than 150 songs and has had several writers adapt lyrics to them. Most of those lyrics are in Hebrew. On May 5, 2007, he appeared for the first time as a singer with a band – featuring 20 of his songs in a special concert held at Tel Aviv's famous pop music venue – Tzavta 1.

Ronn's association with jazz pianist and composer Haim Cotton has led to the inception of the New York Piano Academy – a school and method which is devoted to the teachings of both classical and jazz piano disciplines. Their method defines the common grounds between classical and jazz, and qualifies piano students of all levels in both disciplines. The New York Piano Academy has been open to the public since September, 2005, and is in residence at Manhattan's West End Presbyterian Church on the upper west side.

Ronn Yedidia's first Compact Disc recording entitled, "Yedidia Plays Yedidia," was released in March, 2001 on the Altarus label (AIR-CD-9078). His popular "Lullabye" is featured on EMI Classics' Ahn Trio "Groovebox" CD (2003). In 2008 another Ahn Trio recording was released – this time on the SonyBMG label – entitled "Lullaby For My Favorite Insomniac". It features Yedidia's original composition, "The Song On The Land," as well as two of his trio arrangements of Korean and American popular tunes. In April, 2012 Yedidia's first Naxos CD on the American Classics series has been released – featuring his major clarinet & piano works with clarinetist Alexander Fiterstein. The CD has been broadcast worldwide and presented on NPR's, "All Things Considered."

Yehe Ratzon L'fanecha: May It Be Your Will To Show Favor

In 2018, Yedidia signed an exclusive publishing contract with the Japanese publishing house Muse Press. Subsequently, Muse Press embarked on the gigantic project of printing and distributing all of Ronn Yedidia's solo piano works – which tally over 150 to-date.

All of Yedidia's chamber, orchestral, vocal, choral, ethnic and jazz compositions are currently published and distributed through the publishing company Verse Music, in affiliation with BMI (established in 1987).

Designed by Sharon Esther Lampert, Zazzle Gift Shop

Yehe Ratzon L'fanecha: May It Be Your Will To Show Favor

Bibliographical Note

1995-2015-2025 = 30 YEARS

Thirty years ago, I called the Israeli composer and pianist Ronn Yedidia, who at the time was working with the Sutton Place Synagogue Choir in NYC, and commissioned him to write two new melodies for a Shabbat candle lighting blessing that had been silent for centuries. He said, "Yes!" and in less than a month, he had completed the two gorgeous musical compositions, one traditional and one Hassidic for voice and piano. Our written contract specified that I would be the vocalist and peform the music.

For thirty years, the project was derailed for reasons that require explication. For thirty years, I was unable to complete the project and publish the musical compositions due to the fact I was distracted by other creative projects that were percolating beneath the surface like a volcano, and my extra-body part, my "creative apparatus" went into overdrive with other artistic endeavors: 80+Books!

1995
Ronn and I started this project in 1995
Thirty years ago, Ronn Yedidia gave me a black and white photo that is similar to the sculptor Rodin's "Thinker" with a big head of hair and a half-page biography.

2015
I formatted the book in 2015
Twenty years later, it is my pleasure to include his life's musical works to date. I enjoyed finding our Shabbat compositions under "Vocal Works."
I hope you do too!

2025
I published the book in 2025
Thirty years later, after the publication or more than 80+ of my own books, I published the SHABBAT BLESSINGS.

As you can see by the listing of our life's works, we are both gifted and made many immortal contributions.

I made contributions to science, literature, education, and theology.

NYU honored me with an award for, "Multi-Interdisciplinary Studies."

Sharon Is Here, There, and Everywhere!

Silent Shabbat Blessing For Centuries Is Blessed by Two New Melodies

Musical Works of World Renowned Israeli Composer

Ronn Yedidia

Overview of Published Works
1. Solo Piano
2. Two-Piano Works
3. Piano & Organ Works
4. Miscellaneous Solo Works
5. Chamber Works
6. Vocal Works
7. Jazz Works
8. Ethnic & Klezmer Tunes
9. Orchestral Works

Yehe Ratzon L'fanecha: May It Be Your Will To Show Favor

1. SOLO PIANO

Nocturne No. 7, "Going Back Home" (C# Major) Dedicated to Orna Agustari, 2024

Nocturne No. 6, (Eb minor), Dedicated to Adrian and Laura Weller, 2024

Nocturne No. 5, (F# minor), Dedicated to my cousin Chimchon Menasheroff, 2024

Scherzo No. 5, (B Major), Dedicated to my mother-in-law Emily Grant, 2023-2024

Nocturne No. 4, "To Joe" (A minor), Dedicated to the late Joe Patrych, 2023-2024

Scherzo No. 4, (E minor), 2023

Nocturne No. 3, (E minor, Dedicated to the late Bella Tal, 2023

Scherzo No. 3, (C Major), Dedicated to Ed Bottoms, 2023

Nocturne No. 2, (D Major), Dedicated to My Beloved Subliminal, 2023

Scherzo No. 2, (Ab Major), 2022-2023

Nocturne No. 1, (B minor), Dedicated to Sherry Li, 2022

Scherzo No. 1, (Eb minor) Dedicated to Alex Yedidia, 2021

Impromptu, (F minor), a 60-second work written for pianist Hagai Yodan's recording project of '60-second piano works' by Israeli composers, 2021

24 Preludes of Dusk and Dawn
Dedicated to the memory of my mother Rosa Yedidia 1933-2020, composed 2020-2021:

I. Allegretto scorrevole con mistica (C# minor)
II. Moderato; solitario e desideroso (G# minor)
III. Allegro misterioso (D# Phrygian/Major)
IV. "Rose in the Garden" (Bb Major/C Major)
V. "Fantasia" (G Major/E Major)
VI. "Winds of Destiny" (A minor)
VII. "Dreams" (D Major)
VIII. "Storm of Fate" (G minor)
IX. "The Answer" (Eb minor)
X. "Butterflies" (Gb Major)
XI. "Calling of the Bird" (Bb minor)
XII. "Budding" (F Major)
XIII. "Prayer" (B minor)
XIV. "Before the Snow" (F# minor)
XV. "Fata Morgana" (A Major)
XVI. "Once Upon a Flower" (D minor)
XVII. "Despedida, Diego!" (C minor)
XVIII. "Bubbles" (Ab Major)
XIX. "Never Again!" (F minor)
XX. "Memories" (Db Major)

Silent Shabbat Blessing For Centuries Is Blessed by Two New Melodies

XXI. "Orly" (E minor)
XXII. "Yasemin" (B Major 'Impressionistic')
XXIII. "Windows of Spain; Rest in Peace, Chick!" (B Major)
XXIV. "Oath and After…" (D# minor)

5 of the Preludes - No's I, II, V, VII, VIII - World-premiered by Gila Goldstein, Longy School of Music in Cambridge, MA, March 7th, 2022
Prelude No. XVI was world-premiered by Stephen Beus, New York Piano Academy, December 4th, 2022
Prelude No. IV, world-premiered by Gila Goldstein, Bargemusic in Brooklyn, June 17th, 2023
Prelude No. XXIII, world-premiered by Gila Goldstein, Furman University, South Carolina, October 23rd, 2023
5 Preludes, No's X, XI, XII, XIII, XIV, world-premiered by Gila Goldstein, NewYork Piano Academy, May 19th, 2024

Memoirs (poeme), Dedicated to the memory of my cousin Orit Yedidia-Halperin, 1964-2020, Composed 2020

12 Grand Etudes, Volume II (2012-2020):
Grand Etude No. 13 – (mixed keys), Dedicated to Pnina Salzman, 2012
Grand Etude No. 14 – (A minor), Dedicated to Fei-Ping Hsu, 2014
Grand Etude No. 15 – "The Answer" (B Major/E minor), Dedicated to Elisha Abas, 2014
Grand Etude No. 16 – "Spring Impromptu" (G Major), Dedicated to Gila Goldstein, 2015
World Premiere: Loewe Theatre at NYU, May 7, 2017, by pianist Gila Goldstein
Grand Etude No. 17 – "Flames on the Water" (D minor), Dedicated to Alexei Sultanov, 2016
Grand Etude No. 18 – "Metamorphosis," (F minor/Db Major), Dedicated to Alice & Emma Tahmizian, 2016
Grand Etude No. 19 – (B minor), Dedicated to Natan Brand, 2017
Grand Etude No. 20 – (Db Major), Dedicated to Stephen Beus, 2017
First Performance: Oklahoma State Music Teachers Association, June 3rd, 2022 – by pianist Stephen Beus
Grand Etude No. 21 – "Gospel" (Eb Major), Dedicated to Nathaniel Yangco, 2018
Grand Etude No. 22 – "Unison" (F# minor), Dedicated to Jochem le Cointre, 2018, rewritten in 2020
Grand Etude No. 23 – "Kaleidoscope" (G# Major), Dedicated to Corey Hamm, 2018-2019
Grand Etude No. 24 – "Orit" (Bb minor), Dedicated to Shota Ezaki, 2019

5 Waltzes, 2011-2017
Mia's Dream (Little Fantasy, 2012
Dedicated to Mia Veissid in honor of her Bat-Mitzva celebration, Fantasy, 2007
Commissioned by Mrs. Paula Oreck for pianist Alon Goldstein
World Premiere: University of Oklahoma in Norman, OK, November 9th, 2014 (Stephen Beus, pianist)
Rhapsody, Commissioned by the 2006 San Antonio International Piano Competition
First Performances given by 5 finalists at the San Antonio International Piano Competition, October 2006
Alexey Koltakov – **Winner of Best Performance of Commissioned Work Award**
Piano Sonata No. 6, "Bells of Dawn," 2004

Yehe Ratzon L'fanecha: May It Be Your Will To Show Favor

Nominated for 2005 Van Cliburn International Piano Competition
Dedicated to Emma Tahmizian
First Performance: Weill Recital Hall at Carnegie Hall, March 2007 (Soheil Nasseri, pianist)
European Premiere: Berlin's Konzerthaus, Kleiner Saal, April 2007 (Soheil Nasseri, pianist)

Dances of Earth, Wind and Fire, 1999-2003:
I. Firebirds
II. Hush! Desert Winds…
III. Tribes On Earth
IV. Prelude To The Ocean
V. The Abyss Of Wars
Commissioned by 21st Century Classical
World Premiere: Alice Tully Hall, New York on September 30th, 2003 (Soheil Nasseri, pianist)

The Mission is Impossible, 2002
Commissioned by Mr. Nathaniel Yangco
First Performance: The Americas Society, New York, May 2002 (Nathaniel Yangco, pianist)

12 Preludes for Young Pianists, 2000:
I. The Stroll by the Fountain
II. Wondering by the Sea
III. Open the Gates!
IV. Out on a Spring Day
V. When Will You Return?
VI. Waltz of the Puppet
VII. Orion's Nightmare
VIII. Reflection in a Candle
IX. March of the Gypsies
X. Hear the Echoes
XI. April Winds
XII. The Wonderer

21 Waltzes, 1996-2001
Varied sets premiered at "Sundays on the Island" Music Series, City Island, New York, 1998, and at the Piano Music Teachers' Guild of New Jersey, lecture/recital, 2000

Cadenza for W.A. Mozart's Piano Concerto in C minor, K. 491, 2000
Commissioned by Dr. Ronald Wharton
First Performance: Robbins Auditorium at the Albert Einstein College of Medicine, New York, May 2000 (Ron Wharton, pianist)
Blue and White, 1998
Cool, 1998
Overture, 1997
Stride, 1997
Toward the Gardens of Heaven, 1997, Dedicated to brother and poet Gil Yedidia
First Performances: Carola van den Houten's Soiree in NYC, November 14, 1997
"Sundays on the Island" Music Series, City Island, New York on February 8, 1998
Ballet With the Wind, 1997

Silent Shabbat Blessing For Centuries Is Blessed by Two New Melodies

12 Grand Etudes, Volume I, 1993-1997, and 2002-2006:
Grand Etude No. 1 – (C minor for the right hand), Dedicated to Leon Fleisher
Grand Etude No. 2 – (G Mixolydian), Dedicated to Natasha Tadson
Grand Etude No. 3 – (Eb/F# Major), Dedicated to Marc-Andre Hamelin
Grand Etude No. 4 – "Notturno" (Bb minor), Dedicated to Pnina Salzman
Grand Etude No. 5 – (D Major), Dedicated to Evgeny Kissin
Grand Etude No. 6 – "Sunrise" (A minor), Dedicated to Ilene McKeown
Grand Etude No. 7 – "The Flight Over The Ocean" (F# Major), Dedicated to Arthur Hart
Grand Etude No. 8 – "A Voice is Calling in the Desert at Night" (C# minor), Dedicated to Fiona Grant
Grand Etude No. 9 – "Spring" (E Major), Dedicated to Martha Argerich (Revised: 2021)
Grand Etude No. 10 – "Tempest" (B minor), Dedicated to Ivo Pogorelich
Grand Etude No. 11 – "Tragic" (Ab minor for the left hand), Dedicated to Ronn Yedidia
Grand Etude No. 12 – "Mountain Heights" (F Major), Dedicated to Dan-Wen Wei
Varied sets first performed at Hotel Wales Chamber Music Series, New York, January 1995, Steinway Hall, New York, November 1996

Chanson, 1996
From the Valley, 1996
Ether, 1996
First Performance: Steinway Hall, New York, November 1996
And His Mind Wandered, 1996

12 Preludes for Children, 1994-1996:
I. Raindrops on a Sunny Day
II. The Runaway Music Box
III. Sadness
IV. Dancing in the Snow
V. Toccatina
VI. Longing
VII. Alone in the Mist
VIII. The Dream
IX. The Chase
X. At my Daughter's Piano
XI. Nunu Hears Stories
XII. Israeli Song
First Performance: Steinway Hall, New York, November 1996

Scherzando D'Amore, 1994
Exercise in Common Time, 1994
Impromptu, "Motherland," 1994
Legend, "The River of Love," 1994
Ballade No. 2, 1993
Piano Sonata No. 5, 1991-1992, Dedicated to Marc-Andre Hamelin
World Premiere: Kioi-cho Salon Hall, Tokyo, Japan – on August 5th, 2018, (Shota Ezaki, pianist)
Soliloquy, 1991

Yehe Ratzon L'fanecha: May It Be Your Will To Show Favor

First Performance: Weill Recital Hall at Carnegie Hall, March 2003 (Soheil Nasseri, pianist)

Chorale, 1991

First Performance: Christ & St. Stephen's Church, NewYork City, April 1992

6 Nocturnes, 1991

First Performance: Bloomingdale House of Music, New York, March 1993

7 Short Pieces, 1990

First Performance: B'nai Jeshurun Synagogue, New York, November 1990

Poeme, 1989-1990

Melodie, 1989, Dedicated to Fiona Grant

First Performance: Memorial Auditorium, Louisville, Kentucky, January 1991

(Winner of 1991 New Sounds Competition)

Piano Sonata No. 4, "Treludium," 1988, Dedicated to Joe Patrych

Episode, Etude and Song, 1986

First Performance: B'nai Jeshurun Synagogue, New York, November 1990

Piano Sonata No. 3, "Outcries," Dedicated to Arthur Hart, 1985

First Performances: Paul Hall, Juilliard, Arthur Hart, pianist, May 6, 1986

New Music Weekend at Lincoln Center, Juilliard Theater, Aviva Aranovich, pianist, April 1987

(Winner of Juilliard Composition Competition)

Peery Roads, 1985

First Performance: Memorial Auditorium, Louisville, Kentucky, January 1991

(Winner of 1991 New Sounds Competition)

Chaconne, 1984, (revised 1988)

First Performance: Moscow Conservatory, May 1990

Piano Sonata No. 2, 1983

First Performance: YMCA Hall, Jerusalem, January 1985 (Uriel Tsachor, pianist)

Ballade for the Mournful Moon, Dedicated to Pnina Salzman, 1982

Prophets, 1981

First Performance: Israeli Jazz Festival, Jerusalem, March 1982

Etude No. 2, "Chaplinian," 1977

First Performance: Tel Aviv Museum, May 1977

Piano Sonata No. 1, 1976-1977

I. Allegro con forza

II. Mesto

First Performances:Bruno Walter Auditorium, Lincoln Center, New York on April 14, 1984

(World Premiere, Arthur Hart, pianist)

Gina Bachauer International Piano Competition, Arthur Hart, pianist, 1984

Etude No. 1 (1975)

Silent Shabbat Blessing For Centuries Is Blessed by Two New Melodies

2. TWO-PIANO WORKS
Longa Shahnaz - traditional Lebanese tune, transcribed for 2 pianos, 2016-2017
Perspectives - Homage to Frederic Chopin, 2010
Co-composed with Haim Cotton
First Performance: Merkin Concert Hall, April 2010

3. PIANO & ORGAN WORKS
Symphonic Poem, 2008-10
Commissioned by the Hudson Valley Piano Club for the New York Piano-Organ Duo

4. MISCELLANEOUS SOLO WORKS
Sonata for solo guitar, 2016-18, Commissioned by Ms. Fiona Fein for guitarist Giacomo La Vita:
I.   Moderato ad lib.; Allegretto
II. Andante nobile
III. Presto appassionato

Sparx2 (solo clarinet; 2013)
Commissioned by the Adele and John Gray Endowment of AICF – for clarinetist Alexander Fiterstein

6 Etudes for solo guitar, Commissioned by Ms. Fiona Fein for guitarist Giacomo La Vita, 2011
No. 1 – D minor
No. 2 – E minor/B Major
No. 3 – Eb minor
No. 4 – F Major
No. 5 – G Major/Eb Major
No. 6 – A minor

Sparx, solo clarinet, 2010
Commissioned by the Adele and John Gray Endowment of AICF for clarinetist Alexander Fiterstein
Ballade, solo guitar, 2005
Commissioned by and Dedicated to Giacomo La Vita
First Performance by Giacomo La Vita at the Greenville Community Church Recital Series in New York, February 7, 2010
Lara, solo violin, 2004
Dedicated to Lara St. John
Jubilation, solo organ, 2002
Dedicated to Chris & Mercedes Rice in honor of their wedding
First Performance: Trinity Episcopal Church, Stamford, Connecticut, October 2002
2 Waltzes, solo accordion, 1999, 2001
First Performance: The Unitarian Church of Montclair, NewJersey, October 2001
Chaconne, solo cello, 1995
Dedicated to David Eggar
Fanfare, solo piccolo trumpet, 1995
In memory of Prime Minister Yitzhak Rabin
Awakening, solo violin, 1991-92
Dedicated to Paul Gati
Pluralism 1986, solo bass clarinet, 1986
Dedicated to Bohdan Hilash
First Performance: Sion Contemporary Festival, France, August 1986

Yehe Ratzon L'fanecha: May It Be Your Will To Show Favor

5. CHAMBER WORKS

Niggun for clarinet and piano, 2019, Dedicated to Giora Feidman

Moonstruck (for vibraphone, percussion, and piano, 2011
Co-composed with Yuval Edoot
First Performance: Merkin Concert Hall, April 2011

The Concordians (flute, violin, cello, guitar, and piano), 2011
Commissioned by the Concordia Conservatory of Music & Art

Berceuse (flute, violin, cello, guitar, and piano), 2011

3 Pieces (clarinet and piano), 2010:
I. Impromptu
II. Nocturne
III. World Dance
Commissioned by Dr. & Mrs. Malcolm & Davina Weller
First Performance: Merkin Concert Hall, April 2010

String Trio (violin, viola and cello), 2009-2010
I. Enigma
II. Scherzando
III. Finale
Composed for the Amerigo Trio (Glenn Dicterow, violin; Karen Dreyfus, viola; Inbal Segev, cello)
First Performance: Merkin Concert Hall, April 2010

Nebulight Zone (vibraphone, percussion, and piano, 2008
Co-composed with Yuval Edoot
First Performance: Merkin Concert Hall, May 2008

Sweet, Sweet Rachel (string quartet and piano; 2008, Dedicated to Rachel Weller
First Performance: Merkin Concert Hall, May 2008

Farewell, Nathaniel (clarinet and piano; 2007), In memory of Dr. Nathaniel Yangco, 1975-2007
First Performance: Merkin Concert Hall, May 2008

Trio (clarinet, cello, and piano), Commissioned by the Seattle Chamber Music Society, 2007 Summer Festival, 2007
First Performance: Seattle Chamber Music Society Summer Festival at Lakeside School, July 2007

Concertino (clarinet, string trio, and piano)
Commissioned by Mrs. Paula Oreck for clarinetist Alex Fiterstein
First Performance: Merkin Concert Hall, New York, April 2007

Domm (vibraphone, percussion, and keyboards), 2006-2007
Co-composed with Yuval Edoot
First Performance: Merkin Concert Hall, April 2007

Lyric Trio (flute, cello, and piano; 2006)
First Performance: Merkin Concert Hall, New York, April 2007

String Quartet No. 2, in two movements, 2006:
I. Chorale
II. Danza
Dedicated to the Maia Quartet
First Performance: Merkin Concert Hall, New York, May 2006

Silent Shabbat Blessing For Centuries Is Blessed by Two New Melodies

Fantaisie Concertante (harp, flute, and string quartet), 2006
Commissioned by Mr. Gideon Vaisman for harpist Suzanna Klintcharova
First Performance: Merkin Concert Hall, New York, May 2006

In and Out (vibraphone, percussion, and piano), 2006
Co-composed with Yuval Edoot
First Performance: Merkin Concert Hall, New York, May 2006

Impromptu a Two (vibraphone, percussion, and piano), 2004-2005
Co-composed with Yuval Edoot
First Performances: Christ & St. Stephen's Church, New York, March 2004
Merkin Concert Hall, New York, April 2005

Panorama (cello and piano), 2003
Dedicated to Wanda Glowacka

Presto (violin and cello), 2003
Dedicated to Wolfgang Tsoutsouris & Wanda Glowacka

Ominous Games (2 trumpets, vibraphone, piano, and double bass) 2003
First performance: Christ & St. Stephen's Church NewYork, March 2003

Little Hours of Bliss (violin, cello, and piano) 2002, revised in 2007
Commissioned by the Ahn Trio
First Performance: The Admiral Theatre, Bremerton, Washington, May 2002

Poeme-Fantasie (cello and piano), 2002
Commissioned by the Oklahoma City Community Fund

Waltz (cello and piano), 2002
Commissioned by the Oklahoma City Community Fund

Winter of Birds (2 string quartets, and piano), 2001-2002
First Performance: Christ & St. Stephen's Church, New York, March 2002

Toward the Horizon (string quartet, flute and piano), 2000
First Performance: Christ & St. Stephen's Church, NewYork, April 2000

Between Night and Day (percussion ensemble and piano), 1998
First Performance: Christ & St. Stephen's Church, New York, April 1999

Rondo Macabre (violin and piano), 1997
Dedicated to Wolfgang Tsoutsouris
First Performance: "Sundays on the Island" Music Series, City Island, New York, 1998

Piano Quintet (piano, 2 violins, viola, and cello), 1996-1997
First Performance: Christ & St. Stephen's Church, New York, April 1997

The Song on the Land (bassoon and piano), 1996
(Transcribed for violin, cello, and piano) 2005, For Ahn Trio
First Performance: YMCA Hall, Jerusalem, March 2003

Fantasy (violin and piano), 1996
First Performance: "Sundays on the Island" Music Series, City Island, New York, 1998

Poeme (clarinet and piano), 1995
First Performance: Christ & St. Stephen's Church, New York, April 1996

Fanfare (piccolo trumpet), 1995, In memory of Prime Minister Yitzhak Rabin
(Transcribed for piccolo trumpet, and piano), 2004
First Performance: Merkin Concert Hall, New York, April 2005

Cheers (flute and piano), 1995

Trio No. 1 (violin, cello, and piano), 1994-1995
First Performance: Christ & St. Stephen's Church, New York, April 1995

Nocturne (cello and piano), 1994-1995
Lullabye (cello and piano), 1994
(Transcribed for violin, cello, and piano), 2001, For Ahn Trio

Yehe Ratzon L'fanecha: May It Be Your Will To Show Favor

Vocalise (flute and piano), 1993
First Performance: Christ & St. Stephen's Church, New York, April 1994
Encore (violin and piano), 1993
First Performance: Late Night Show, Hartford TV, October 1993
When Will I See You Again? (flute and piano), 1993
(Transcribed for violin, cello, and piano), 2003
First Performance: Merkin Concert Hall, New York, May 2006
Elegy (violin and piano), 1991-1993
First Performance: Christ & St. Stephen's Church, New York, April 1993
Trio No. 2 (flute, clarinet, and piano), 1992
First Performance: Christ & St. Stephen's Church, NewYork, December 1992
"Black Snow" (flute, clarinet, and piano), 1986
First Performances:
Society for New Music in Syracuse, New York, February 1989
(Winner of 1988 Brian Israel Award)
Alice Tully Hall, May 1989 (Winner of Juilliard Composition Competition)
Tableaux Decousus (alto flute, bass clarinet, and piano), 1986
3 Light Pieces (clarinet, piano, and synthesizers), 1985
Pyramids (bass, clarinet, and piano), 1985
Symbolism 1985 (two flutes), 1985
First Performance: University of Alberta, Edmonton, Canada, January 1986
Suite for Flute and Piano, in four movements, 1983-1984
First Performance: Festival of the Atlantic, New Jersey, August 1990
Seclusion (violin and piano), 1983

String Quartet No. 1 in two movements, 1982-1983:
I. Grave
II. Moderato; Allegro
First Performance: Leonia United Methodist Church, Leonia,New Jersey, October 2001
Introduction and Scherzo (violin and piano), 1980

6. VOCAL WORKS

203 Songs in popular & ethnic styles, 1995-2024
First Performance of 15 songs: Temple Israel, Great Neck, New York, February 2000
Various sets premiered at Merkin Concert Hall, New York, in 2005, 2006, 2007, 2008, 2010, and 2011
20 songs premiered at Tzavta, Tel Aviv, May 5, 2007
12 songs premiered at the Rozin Auditorium, Tel Aviv, July 29, 2019

"Danny Dan" (Nocturne for soprano & guitar, music & lyrics by Ronn Yedidia, 2012-2013
In memory of Ronn's cousin, Danny Grinberg, 1959-2011
Written for Jeanai & Giacomo La Vita on the occasion of their debut CD
First Performance: Greenville Community Church, Scarsdale, NY, February 2013

"Modim Anachnu Lach," from the Jewish prayer (baritone, S.A.T.B. choir, cello and piano), 2008
Commissioned by Cantor Raphael Frieder
First Performance: Merkin Concert Hall, May 2008

"Mi Sheberach," from the Jewish prayer (baritone, S.A.T.B. choir (oboe, cello, and piano), 2005
Commissioned by Temple Israel of Great Neck: Dedicated to Cantor Raphael Frieder
First Performances: Temple Israel of Great Neck, Long Island, September 2005
Merkin Concert Hall, New York, May 2006

Silent Shabbat Blessing For Centuries Is Blessed by Two New Melodies

Music for 7 biblical texts, Co-composed with George Cavalieri:
"Songs of Worship," Revelation 5 (chorus and piano), 2007
"A Song for the Nations," Psalm 67 (chorus and piano), 2007
"A Prayer of Moses – the Man of God," Psalm 90 (chorus and piano), 2005
"The Song of Moses and the Lamb," Revelation 15, (chorus and piano), 2006
"Song of the Multitude from Every Nation" Revelation 7:9-12, (baritone, chorus and piano), 2005
"Think On These Things," Philippians 4:8 (chorus and piano), 2005
"Give Thanks," Jeremaiah 33:11 (chorus and piano), 2004, Commissioned by Mr. George Cavalieri
As Long as the Candle Is Lit (S.A.T.B. choir and piano), 2003, Commissioned by the Zamir Chorale
First Performance: Merkin Concert Hall, New York, March 2005
The Pond (voice & piano), 1996
"Tov Lehodot," from the Jewish prayer (mezzo soprano and piano), 1995-1996
First Performance: Christ & St. Stephen's Church, New York, March 2004
"Shema," from the Jewish prayer (mezzo soprano and piano), 1996

A SILENT PRAYER FOR CENTURIES HAS A VOICE!

"Yehi Ratson," from the Jewish prayer, two versions in a popular style (voice and piano), 1995
Commissioned by Ms. Sharon Esther Lampert

The Song on Crossing the Red Sea, "Shirat HaYam" (6 movements, for baritone and piano), 1990
Commissioned by Mr. Amos Schulberg, by Prana (soprano voice and bass clarinet), 1986
First Performance: NYU Festival, May 1986

7 JAZZ WORKS

And the Day has Come (for Prophets' 3rd Stream Trio and Marc Stocker, piano/synth, bass, and drums), 2024
Ping Pong (piano trio), 2024
Middle of the Road (piano trio), 2023
Dudu Kedem, Dedicated to my buddy and hero David Kedem (piano trio), 2023
First Performance: Connolly's Klub 45, New York, March 2023
If I Were a Julius (piano trio), 2022
First Performance: The Delancey, New York, January 2023
Never Landed (piano trio or sax, piano, bass, and drums), 2022
First Performance: The Delancey, New York, January 2023
Ma'alesh (piano trio), 2022
Just Like That (piano trio), 2020
Ronndo (piano trio), 2019-20
Love Not Easy (piano trio), Dedicated to Keith Jarrett, 2017
Puzzle (piano trio), 2017
First Performance: Bernie Wohl Center, New York, May 2018
Yossi Cohen Is Life, Dedicated to my best buddy, the late Yossi Cohen (piano trio), 2016
First Performance: The Delancey, New York, January 2023
Joke (piano trio), 2015
First Performance: The 55 Bar, New York, February 2018
Flashback (for flute, piano, bass, and drums), 2015
First Performance: The 55 Bar, New York, February 2018
I Thought So, Dedicated to the great Robin Williams (piano trio), 2014
First Performance: The 55 Bar, New York, February 2018

Yehe Ratzon L'fanecha: May It Be Your Will To Show Favor

I Thought So, Dedicated to the great Robin Williams (piano trio), 2014
First Performance: The 55 Bar, New York, February 2018
You (piano trio), 2013
Train To The Moon (piano trio), 2013
If Ever (flute, piano, bass and drums), 2013
First Performance: West End Presbyterian Church, New York, May 2014
Sharp Haze (piano trio), 2012-13
First Performance: West End Presbyterian Church, New York, May 2014
EX-Rays (flute, piano, bass and drums), 2012-13
First Performance: West End Presbyterian Church, New York, May 2014
Carry On (flute, piano, bass, and drums), 2011
First Performance: West End Presbyterian Church, New York, May 2014
Funking (flute, piano, bass, and drums), 2011
First Performance: West End Presbyterian Church, New York, May 2014
Quest (flute, piano, bass, and drums; 1996 (revised 2011)
First Performance: West End Presbyterian Church, New York, May 2014
Your Song (piano trio), 2009
Dedicated to Keith Jarrett
Seesaw (piano trio), 2007
Jazz Time (piano trio), 2007
Boppin' (piano trio), 2004)
U.N.I., Co-composed with Yuval Edoot (piano, vibraphone, bass, and drums), 2004
Bittersweet (piano trio), 2004
First Performance: Bernie Wohl Center, New York, May 2018
Night Standard (piano trio), 2003
Orion In The Sky And On My Earth, Dedicated to my beloved boy Orion (piano trio), 1998
First Performance: The 55 Bar, New York, February 2018
The Other Side Of The Road, Dedicated to my musician friend Richard Thompson; (piano trio), 1998
A Journey To Nowhere (flute, piano, bass, and drums), 1994
Soul Seeks A Place (flute, piano, bass, and drums), 1994
Timeless Night (flute, piano, bass, and drums), 1993
Brazilian Dream (flute, piano, bass, and drums), 1992
And Love For All (flute, piano, bass, and drums), 1992
Melodie, Dedicated to my gorgeous wife Fiona; (solo piano), 1989, revised and arranged for (flute, piano, bass, and drums), 2011
First Performance: Memorial Auditorium, Louisville, Kentucky, January 1991
(Winner of 1991 New Sounds Competition)
Ballade (flute, piano, bass, and drums), 1988
Superfusion (flute, piano, bass, and drums), 1986-88
Variations on Four Jazz Tunes (flute, piano, bass, and drums),1985
Meira (Dedicated to my beloved mother-in-law Meira Yatsiv, (flute, piano, bass, and drums), 1984
Streams (flute, piano, bass, and drums), 1983
Arabesque (flute, piano, bass, and drums), 1983
Horizons (flute, piano, bass, and drums), 1982-1983
Landscapes (flute, piano, bass, and drums), 1982
Shallow Water (electric piano, acoustic piano, bass, and drums), 1981
First Performance: Israeli Jazz Festival, Jerusalem, March 1982
Prophets (piano, flute, bass, and drums), 1981
First Performance: Israeli Jazz Festival, March 1982 (selected amongst the winning compositions at the festival, and performed at the Jerusalem Theater during the final event which was broadcast live on Israel's National Radio

Silent Shabbat Blessing For Centuries Is Blessed by Two New Melodies

8. ETHNIC AND KLEZMER TUNES

For Ukraine (accordion, guitar, bass, and percussion), 2022, World-premiered on solo accordion by Ronn Yedidia at The Center at West Park in Manhattan, March 19, 2022

KlezDance No. 14, "Debka Blues" (accordion, violin, guitar, bass, and percussion), 2015

KlezDance No. 13, "Thalassaki and The Little Shepherd" (accordion, flute/violin, guitar, bass, and percussion), Dedicated to Ronn's mother, Rosa Yedidia, 2013

KlezDance No. 12 (KlezJazz), "Round and Round" (accordion, flute/violin, guitar, bass, and percussion) Dedicated to Ronn's mother, Rosa Yedidia, 2013

KlezDance No. 11, "The Magic Flute" (flute, accordion, violin, guitar, bass, and percussion), 1997 and 2013

First Performance with DanzaNova and flutist Marc Stocker: Baruch Performing Arts Center, NYC, February 2013

KlezDance No. 10, "Flying Gypsy Polka No. 2 (solo accordion or with ensemble), 2012

KlezDance No. 9, "Desert Winds" (accordion, violin, guitar, bass, and percussion), 2011

First Performance with DanzaNova: Merkin Concert Hall, April 2011

KlezDance No. 8 (accordion, guitar, and ensemble; 2011

KlezDance No. 7, "Mazurka" (solo accordion or with ensemble), 2009

KlezDance No. 6, "Flying Gypsy Polka" (solo accordion or with ensemble), 2009

First Performance with Polkastra: Le Poisson Rouge, New York, September 2009

KlezDance No. 5, "Ragtime Polka" (solo piano or with ensemble), 2009

KlezDance No. 4, "Celtic Kalkadunga Polka" (accordion, violin, didgeridoo, bass, and percussion), 2009

First Performance with Polkastra: Le Poisson Rouge, New York, September 2009

KlezDance No. 3 (solo accordion or with ensemble), 2008

First Performance with DanzaNova: Arts Echo Galleria, Union City, New Jersey, December 2008

KlezDance No. 2 (solo accordion or with ensemble), 2008

First Performance with DanzaNova: ArtsEcho Galleria, Union City, New Jersey, December 2008

KlezDance No. 1 (solo accordion or with ensemble), 2005

First Performance with DanzaNova: ArtsEcho Galleria, Union City, New Jersey, December 2008

2 Waltzes (solo accordion or with ensemble), 2002 and 2003

First Performance: The Unitarian Church of Montclair, New Jersey, September 2004

Yehe Ratzon L'fanecha: May It Be Your Will To Show Favor

9. ORCHESTRAL WORKS

Symphony No. 1 in G# minor, "Netzach Yisra'el" ("The Eternity of Israel," 2013-2014
I. Allegretto alla marcia
II. Allegretto scherzando ("Rain Dance")
III. Adagio divino
IV. Allegro brioso
Written for conductor Dalia Atlas

Violin Concerto in A minor, "The Silken Violin," Dedicated to violinist Paul Gati, 2009-2021
1st movement: Allegretto e molto sensibile, 2009, Commissioned by the Tel Aviv Museum
World Premiered on April 13, 2010 at the Tel Aviv Museum with solo violinist Wagner
Luiz Rodrigues & the Israel Chamber Orchestra (abbreviated version)
2nd movement: Adagio, 2010-2012
3rd movement: Allegro ma non troppo, "Mother's Outcry," 2020-2021

World Dance (2010, orchestrated for solo clarinet & symphony orchestra in 2012
World Premiered on October 16, 2012 by clarinetist Alexander Fiterstein and the
University of South Carolina Symphony Orchestra under the baton of Prof. Donald
Portnoy at USC's Kroger Center for the Arts

Fantaisie Concertante (solo harp, flute and string orchestra), 2006
Commissioned by Mr. Gideon Vaisman for harpist Suzanna Klintcharova
First Performance: Young Soloists of New York Chamber Orchestra, Conductor Kiril Tarpo
Symphony Space, New York, June 2006

Steps in the Wonderland, symphonic work, 1997-1998
First Performance: Christ & St. Stephen's Church, New York, March 1998
4 Performances by the Israel Philharmonic Orchestra during the IPO's 70th Anniversary
concert season, Conductor George Pehlivanian, Jerusalem's Congress Center,
Tel Aviv's Mann Auditorium, Haifa's Auditorium, May 2007

Concerto for Piano, Electronic Instruments, Choir and Orchestra, 1989-1990
Commissioned by Dr. Joseph Bookstein
First Performances:
Sherwood Auditorium, La Jolla, California, July 1990 (Ken Bookstein, pianist)
Alice Tully Hall, New York, May 1991, (Ken Bookstein, pianist)

Verses (solo flute and orchestra), 1984-1985
Dedicated to Ed Bottoms

"When I'm
not **writing**
I'm **reading**.
When I'm not **writing**
or **reading**
I'm **singing**."

Sharon Esther Lampert

ABOUT
PRINCESS KADIMAH
VOCALIST AND 8TH PROPHETESS OF ISRAEL
SHARON ESTHER LAMPERT

"It is not enough to tell people what not to do;
It is also important to tell people what to do"

30 COMMANDMENTS
ALL YOU WILL EVER NEED TO KNOW ABOUT GOD
A UNIVERSAL MORAL COMPASS
FOR ALL PEOPLE, ALL RELIGIONS , AND ALL TIME

SHARON ESTHER LAMPERT
PRINCESS KADIMAH
8TH PROPHETESS OF ISRAEL

SharonEstherLampert.com

YOU HAD TO OUTDO MOSES

30 COMMANDMENTS
A Universal Moral Compass For All People, For All Religions, and For All Time

My father, Abraham Lampert's nickname was **BEZALEL** "In the Shadow of God" Chief Architect of the Covenant. I Inherited the Blessing." Exodus: 31:3

1. **LIFE** Over Death
2. **STRENGTH** Over Weakness
3. **DEED** Over Sin
4. **LOVE** Over Hatred
5. **TRUTH** Over Lie
6. **COURAGE** Over Fear
7. **OPTIMISM** Over Pessimism
8. **GRATITUDE** Over Grivances
9. **PATIENCE** Over Frustration
10. **SHARING** Over Selfishness
11. **PRAISE** Over Criticism
12. **RESPONSIBILITY** Over Blame
13. **REWARD** Over Punishment
14. **FORGIVENESS** Over Revenge
15. **UNDERSTANDING** Over Intolerance
16. **ALLIES** Over Enemies
17. **LOYALTY** Over Abandonment
18. **CREATION** Over Destruction
19. **INDIVIDUALITY** Over Conformity
20. **EDUCATION** Over Ignorance
21. **EXCELLENCE** Over Mediocrity
22. **COOPERATION** Over Competition
23. **FREEDOM** Over Oppression
24. **COMPASSION** Over Indifference
25. **FRESH START** Righting Wrongs
26. **HARD WORK** Over Instant Gratification
27. **GOD WITHIN** Over God Above
    GOD IS GO! DO!
28. **INNER PEACE** Over Insane World
29. **JOY** Over Suffering
30. **AWAKE** Over Unconscious

SHARON ESTHER LAMPERT
KADIMAH
8TH PROPHETESS OF ISRAEL

Silent Shabbat Blessing For Centuries Is Blessed by Two New Melodies

MY LOVE OF JEWISH MUSIC
Sharon Esther Lampert

I am never at a loss for words but where should I begin to take you down the long and winding road of my Jewish childhood in America, in and out of five divergent but overlapping stratas of Jewish life: Reform, Conservative, Orthodox, Chabad, and Israeli. It is not easy to be everywhere at once, because each group has their own particular melody for the same song and prayer. And so it goes:

1. I was raised in the Jewish Theological Conservative movement and graduated from the first Robert Gordis Solomon Schecter Day School of Belle Harbor, NYC.
   What an honor!

2. I taught in afternoon Hebrew Schools in the Conservative and Reform movements.
   What an honor!

3. I davened for 18 years with RAMAZ Women's Tefillah, the Orthodox movement on the east side of Manhattan, NYC. A big hug and kiss for our leader Riva Alper.
   What an honor!

4. I was taught how to chant Torah and Haftorah in the Orthodox movement under the stewardship of **MENSCH Cantor Sherwood Goffin** of Lincoln Square Synagogue on the west side of Manhattan, NYC.
   What an honor!

5. I love Israeli music and try to stay up-to-date thanks to my friend Zvi Muskal.
   What an honor!

6. I harbored a fantasy that came true of singing on a float in the **Israeli Day Parade**, Fifth Ave.
   What an honor!

7. I was hired as a vocalist by the **ASHIRA Orchestra Band** by Rabbi Barry Melman to perform at fabulous Jewish holiday parties, see YOUTUBE video.
   What an honor!

The Silent Shabbat Candle Lighting Blessing of Jewish Matriachs

I was first introduced to the silent Shabbat candle lighting blessing in RAMAZ, an Orthodox synagogue, and loved the blessing, but was frustrated that it was a silent blessing, not adorned by a beautiful melody. The blessing was the very first prayer I had ever uttered that made mention of the three ancestral Jewish matriachs, as follows:

> **"Please, hear my supplication at this time, in the merit of Sarah, Rebecca, Rachel and Leah, our Mothers"**

At the time, the Orthodox Jewish women's movement had begun to raise their voices to demand more rights and responsibilities in the synagogue as separate but equal partners in Jewish life; and they achieved success in establishing their own Shabbat services wherein they would read the Torah and Haftorah and **DIY: The Entire Shabbat Service.**

Yehe Ratzon L'fanecha: May It Be Your Will To Show Favor

18 Years Davening with Ramaz NYC
Perhaps it was the intimacy of the small group of Orthodox Jewish women conducting their own sevice in a small chapel off the main drag that first intrigued me, and of course, I loved the Orthodox Jewish musicality and chanting of prayers and their fevor in their davening that held my attention... And so here I stayed for 18 years chanting Torah, Haftorah, and Kiddish and eventually earned the nickname, "Sharon HAGBAHAH Lampert" since as a lefty, I was relied on to hold the Torah upright, when x-heavy on one side at the end of the year.
What an honor!

And there were many more honors bestowed upon me:
Another great memory is that when I didn't participate in the service, and RAMAZ congregants (including the men), let me know that they were dissappointed, because they came just to see me daven. Or when Orthodox RAMAZ men leave their service to hear me daven downstairs, and the Orthodox men have to sit in the back of the room.
What an honor!

From New York to New Jersey, My Davening Traveled
On more than one occassion, Ramaz parents asked me to help out and participate in the Bat-Mitzvah, and read the Haftorah and Kiddish for their daughters. **What an honor!**
I later received a phone call from Jeffery Bernstein, a friend from New Jersey, and he told me that my wonderful davening is the talk of the congregants from New Jersey who attended the Bat-Mitzvah in New York City.
What a surprise!

From time to time, I also participated in the Conservative Park Ave. Synagogue service singing Kiddish for the singles service, (YOUTUBE video).
What an honor!

Job: Second Cantor, Congregation Habonim, NYC
One of my fondest memories was when I saw a small ad in THE JEWISH WEEK for a "Second Cantor," and decided to send in a tape recording of my Kiddish. At the time, it seemed ridiculous because there are Cantorial schools full of qualified male and female candidates. In a bizarre twist of fate, I received a call from the Cantor to audition, and so I set a date. The Rabbi and Cantor went to the back of the synagogue and I chanted the Kiddish. They told me that they prefer my mezzo-soprano voice to the sopranos and gave me fifty pages to music to learn that deviated from both the Orthodox and Conservative melodies, and was modern Reform music. I was offered a real job as a "**Second Cantor**," with a conservative synagogue singing reform liturgy on the west side of Manhattan. I regret not taking the cantorial job. **What an honor!** I was already buried in my 80+ books, and unable to balance both callings!

Bat-Mitzvah Revolution: Friday to Saturday Mornings and Orthodox Women Rise Up
At my own Bat-Mitzvah, Conservative Jewish women were not allowed to read Torah, but were allowed to read the Haftorah on Saturday mornings. After my reading, I was so happy I reached over and planted a kiss on Rabbi Allen Blaine's cheek, and the entire congregation burst out laughing. My Orthodox neighbors, Beth and Eden Nussbawm enjoyed the service, so much so, that soon after the service, they spoke to their Orthodox Rabbi demanding an Orthodox Women's Bat-Mitzvah service of their own. After the big Bat-Mitzvah day, whenever I entered the synagogue, there was an elderly gentleman who always had my prayerbook opened to the right page, and handed it to me as soon as I entered the room. I never again had to open a prayerbook or find the right page.
What an honor!

Silent Shabbat Blessing For Centuries Is Blessed by Two New Melodies

Jewish Education Float, NYC, 5TH AVE.
My most favorite day was when my childhood fantasy came true, and I was chosen to be the singing sensation on the Jewish Education Float during the Israeli Day Parade marching down fabulous Fifth Ave. After a few phone calls, they agreed that I should NOT look like a Hebrew school teacher, but as a STARLET, and wear a gorgeous sexy dress. It was a childhood dream come true! Cautious: I packed two dresses just in case they decide to reverse their decision).
What an honor!

ISRAELI DAY PARADE JEWISH EDUCATION FLOAT, FIFTH AVE, NYC

For more then 10 years, I taught adults and children in afternoon Hebrew school programs, and pioneered the program, "In One Hour, Learn to Read Hebrew." A photo of my adult B'nai-Mitzvah class is published in a book by Susan Schneiderman called, "Jewish and Female."
What an honor!

One of the greatest honors was being asked to prepare a deaf student for her Bat-Mitzvah. She could read lips, and was holding her own in a school with hearing students, and doing very well academically.
What an honor!

There are Jewish kids in afternoon Hebrew school programs still memorizing their Haftorah portions, and do not learn to read Hebrew. The excuse is that there is no TIME to teach kids to read Hebrew. I solved this problem! My class: "In One Hour, Learn to Read Hebrew."

My Afternoon Hebrew School Teacher Resume:
1. Reform Steven Wise Free Synagogue: Adults and Children (Received Service Award by Rabbi Balfour Brickner)
2. Reform Temple Emanu-El (Published a Book of Ardent Fan Letters from Rabbi David Posner)
3. Reform Temple Israel: Rabbi Judy Lewis
4. Conservative Sutton Place Synagogue: Adults and Children's High-Holiday Services

Yehe Ratzon L'fanecha: May It Be Your Will To Show Favor

I have fond memories of the men from the Sutton Place Synagogue senior center, who held their meetings at the same time as the afternoon Hebrew school classes; and who would stop by my class and stick their heads in for a brief moment and say, "If my Hebrew teacher looked like you, I would have been a Rabbinic scholar!" This remark had followed me around for years and I heard other male teachers repeat the same idea to school principals, "The reason her kids know how to read Hebrew, is that she is cute! so the kids listen to her."

I was hired by an Israeli woman going through a divorce to a a gentile spouse to teach her son to read Hebrew in preparation for his Bar-Mitzvah. He was six years old at the time. She told him, "You have a beautiful teacher, so pay attention, and learn to read Hebrew." It was the first time a woman was using my glamour for educational purposes to motivate her six year old child, LOL!

And so, the Jewish world in which I live is rich in diversity as it is inclusive of all Jewish denominations of Orthodox, Conservative, Reform, CHABAD and ISRAELI Jews. I live my life as a "RE-CONSERVA-DOX." I am the only member of the group; and it is a great spiritual challenge because I have to like everybody: Reform, Conservadox, and Orthodox Jews.

Another interesting highlight comes to mind, when I was hired to prepare a non-denominational Jewish boy for his Bar-Mitzvah. In this particular case, the parents refused to join any group and asked me to perform the Bar-Mitzvah at a "Jewish Science" ceremony. Behind the scenes, the parents were on the verge of divorce due to the infighting, and the Holocaust survivor grandparents refused to come to the ceremony. SCHMALTZY my beloved cat-child saved the day, when they saw him wearing an infant's KIPPAH on his head. They all laughed at the cat and realized that wearing a KIPPAH was NO BIG DEAL even for a cat. If SCHMALTZY the cat could wear a KIPPAH, without resistance; then their son could also wear a KIPPAH. This story is beautifully illustrated in SCHMALTZY's children's book entitled, "SCHMALTZY: In America, Even a Cat Can Have a Dream, The First Children's Book with Color-Coded Vocabulary Words."

FALAFEL (left) and the Piano Playing SCHMALTZY (right)

Silent Shabbat Blessing For Centuries Is Blessed by Two New Melodies

My Unexhibited Holocaust Ceramic Tile

Another story I hold dear to my heart, is when children of the Sutton Place Synagogue afternoon school were asked by the **Holocaust Museum in Washington, D.C**, to create ceramc tiles that depicted Jewish themes to be displayed at an exhibit. As I was the only child of a Holocaust survivor of the school, I decided to participate and create a ceramic tile too! I later wrote poetry to accompany the tile. Since I was not a child, my tile was not included nor sent to the museum. So here it is:

SACRED FEATHERS OF DIVINE FREEDOMS

On the left is a tree deeply rooted in the ground and a bird is dropping its feathers down to the child imprisoned behind the barbwired fence in the Concentration Camp. The child is placing the birds feathers on his clothing in an attempt to fly out of of the Concentration Camp. The bird is helping the Jewish child escape the Holocaust Concentration Camp.

Yehe Ratzon L'fanecha: May It Be Your Will To Show Favor

2015 UPDATE

2015: This year, I am devoted to publishing all of my life's literary works, and decided that my first priority would be to publish the two Jewish musical compositions written 20 years ago, that give the beautiful silent candle lighting blessing a brand new melodious voice.

I can't believe twenty years have passed since these two musical compositions were written by Ronn Yedidia. I apologize to Ronn Yedidia for the twenty-year derailment, but I know that he is also working on a myriad of music compositions, and intimately understands the creative process that I formalized in a book entitled, "Unleash the Creator, The God Within, The Ten Esoteric Laws of Genius and Creativity."

Fortunately, after 20 years, I revisited Ronn Yedidia's website and downloaded his ten page bibliography, that was only **HALF A PAGE** when I first met him, and of course, he also had a big **HEAD OF HAIR** (see photo).

I am so delighted to be able to publish our creative works together in the appendix for future generations, since artists are mortal, but VESSELS; and ART IS IMMORTAL and will touch the future for Jewish generations to come.

As I write these words, Ronn has no idea that he is about to receive a fabulous surprise of seeing his gorgeous musical compositions published for online downloads and sent to Jewish music librairies.

I was happy to see my name at the bottom of in his enormous bibliography, since we have both spent out lives fulfilling our potential as gifted prodigies.

In sum, I want to acknowledge my EGALITARIAN conservative Jewish upbringing, at the Jewish Theological Seminary of America, because it was here that the seeds were planted for women to become equal partners in Jewish life, and in all personal and professional arenas of life including academics, sports, and the arts.

In childhood, I was able to out run most boys in sports, and continued to do so as as adult, having been born like a high-strung thoroughbred race horse. I never married, because, I have very long legs and no one was able to catch me, LOL!

As for children, my womb malfunctioned, and I was only able to give birth to PURRFECT kittens, SCHMALTZY and FELAFEL, LOL!

SCHMALTZY loves Jewish music and always sits on my desk while I practice, and even enjoys volunteering his long sinuous body as the book rest for my prayerbook.

METAPHYSICAL: In a bizarre twist of fate, I brought home a child's toy piano that I rescued from the trash on 82nd street right in front of my apartment, and SCHMALTZY immediately sat down in front of the keyboard and knew exactly what to do, and started to play the piano and became a WORLD FAMOUS VIRTUOSO, visit SCHMALTZY.com, YOUTUBE video.

Silent Shabbat Blessing For Centuries Is Blessed by Two New Melodies

What Happens When You Dress Up Albert Einstein As Marilyn Monroe?
SHARON ESTHER LAMPERT

Honors & Awards

NYU AWARD
Multi-Interdisciplinary Studies
NYU 3 Degrees: BA, MA, MA
NYU Varsity Basketball Team
NYU Weightlifting Contest

NYC AWARD
100 Year Scholarship Award
Presented by NYC Mayor Koch

NY EMPIRE STATE AWARD
Math and Science Scholarship

JERUSALEM FELLOWSHIP
Aish Hatorah, Israel

ROCKEFELLER UNIVERSITY
Neuroscience Paper Publication

FIRST PRIZE
Upper East Side Resident
Newspaper Writing Contest

FIRST PRIZE
THE WAVE (1893) Art Contest

#1 POETRY WEBSITE
For Student Poetry Projects

POETRY WORLD RECORD
120 Words of Rhyme from
One Family of Rhyme
First Woman to Write a Book
on 5000 Years of Jewish History
Using 6 Poetic Refrains

The IDEA of Sharon Esther Lampert was born in ISRAEL.
For Sharon to be born, her mother and father traveled to ISRAEL, met, and married.
Her mother and father spoke to each other in Yiddish with Russian backgrounds.
Four languages were spoken at home: English, Hebrew, Yiddish, and Russian.

Yehe Ratzon L'fanecha: May It Be Your Will To Show Favor

CONTRIBUTIONS TO CIVILIZATION
Scientist, Artist, Educator, Peacemaker

Published 80+ Books
NYU: PERSTARE et PRAESTARE

PRODIGY
10 Esoteric Laws of Genius and Creativity
Awesome Art of Alliteration Using One Letter of the Alphabet
THE WHY CHILD: Questions Asked and Answered

PROPHET
GOD IS GO! DO!
22 COMMANDMENTS: A UNIVERSAL MORAL COMPASS

PHYSICIST
LAWS OF INEXTRICABILITY

PSYCHOBIOLOGIST
THE SPERM MANIFESTO: 10 RULES FOR THE ROAD

PHILOSOPHER QUEEN
The Philosophy of Love: ME and WE
The Philosophy of Evil; THE DOUBLE WHAMMY
Women Have All The Power But Have Never Learned How to Use It

POET
WORLD POETRY RECORD
120 Words of Rhyme from One Family of Rhyme
#1 Poetry Website for Student Projects
The Greatest Poems Ever Written on Extraordinary World Events
First Woman to Write a Book on 5000 Years of Jewish History in 6 Poetic Refrains

PALADIN OF EDUCATION
SMARTGRADES BRAIN POWER REVOLUTION
8 Goalposts of Education
40 Universal Gold Standards of Education
SCHMALTZY: The First Book of Color-Coded Words
Learn to Read Hebrew in One Hour

PSYCHIATRIST
LOVE YOU MORE THAN YESTERDAY: 14 Relationship Strategies for Happily Ever After
Interpersonal-Integration Therapy to Rebuild the Broken Wings of Students

PEACEMAKER
WORLD PEACE EQUATION
3 Stages of Child Abuse
40 Rules of Manhood: 14 Global Catastrophes of Violence Against Women

PINUP
SEXIEST GENIUS IN HUMAN HISTORY

Published 80+ Books

GENIUS: THE GIFT OF DIVINE REVELATION

MY BOOKS WRITE THEMSELVES

I Am Mortal
MY BOOKS ARE IMMORTAL
Please Handle My Books Gently
My Books Are My Remains

30 Year Project: Shabbat Blessings
Part 1. Birth of Idea: 1995
Part 2. Format Book: 2015
Part 3. Publish Book: January 2025

Also By The Genius

1. Many Jews Reclaimed God, In 5 Minutes Learn 5000 Years of Jewish History
2. TOHO VAVOHU: SIMCHAT TORAH, October 7, 2023
3. POETRY JEWELS: THE GREATEST POEMS EVER WRITTEN ON EXTRAORDINARY JEWISH WORLD EVENTS, #1 Poetry Website for Student Projects, WorldFamousPoems.com
4. 17 HOURS: The First Women in the World in a Tank Battle

Sharon Esther Lampert
SEE THE WORLD THROUGH THE EYES OF A CREATIVE GENIUS
Prodigy, Prophet, Philosopher, Poet, Peacemaker, Paladin of Education, Physicist, Princess
PHOTON SUPERHERO OF EDUCATION and PINUP

FANS@SharonEstherLampert.com

www.ingramcontent.com/pod-product-compliance
Lightning Source LLC
LaVergne TN
LVHW072128060526
838201LV00071B/4996